HOTTER THAN EGYPT

I0139756

Yussef El Guindi

BROADWAY PLAY PUBLISHING INC
New York
www.broadwayplaypublishing.com
info@broadwayplaypublishing.com

Cover art by Andrew Skwish

First edition: November 2023
I S B N: 978-0-88145-990-6

Book design: Marie Donovan
Page make-up: Adobe InDesign
Typeface: Palatino

DEDICATION

To Chris Coleman, John Langs, and Nakissa Etemad for shepherding this play from workshop to full productions. Every playwright should have such artists in their corner.

Including: Wasim No'Mani, who has been with this play from its first staged reading to all three initial productions. Thank you!

HOTTER THAN EGYPT was produced at ACT, Seattle (John Langs, Artistic Director; Anita Shah, Managing Director), opening on 28 January 2022. The cast and creative contributors were:

PAUL .... Paul Morgan Stetler
SEIF ....Wasim No'mani
MAHA ....Naseem Etemad
JEAN ....Jen Taylor
BOATMAN/ MUSEUM GUARD/ DOORMAN
                                                                    Ahmad Kamal

Understudies:
PAUL ....Frank Lawler
SEIF...Ahmad Kamal
MAHA ....Vahishta Vafadari
JEAN ....Candace Vance
BOATMAN/ MUSEUM GUARD/ DOORMAN
                                                                Nima Rakhshanifar

Director...John Langs
Dramaturg.. Nakissa Etemad
Set design.. Carey Wong
Lighting design...Robert J Aguilar
Sound design.. Johanna Melamed
Costume design.. Melanie Burgess
Composer...Nihan Yesil
Dialect coach .... Lynne Soffer
Intimacy and fight director ....Ian Bond
Production stage manager .... Tori Thompson
Production assistant .... David Hsieh
Core company liaison.............................. Lindsey Welliver

HOTTER THAN EGYPT was produced at Marin Theatre Company (Jasson Minadakis, Artistic Director; Meredith Suttles, Managing Director, Nakissa Etemad, Associate Artistic Director), opening on 31 March 2022. The cast and creative contributors were:

PAUL .... Paul Morgan Stetler
SEIF .... Wasim No'mani
MAHA .... Naseem Etemad
JEAN .... Jen Taylor
BOATMAN/ MUSEUM GUARD/ DOORMAN
                                                          Ahmad Kamal

Director .... John Langs
Dramaturg .... Nakissa Etemad
Set design .... Carey Wong
Lighting design .... Jeff Rowlings
Sound design .... Johanna Melamed
Costume design .... Melanie Burgess
Composer .... Nihan Yesil
Dialect coach .... Lynne Soffer
Intimacy and fight director ....Ian Bond
Production stage manager ....Michael Suenkel

HOTTER THAN EGYPT was produced at the Denver Center For The Performing Arts Theatre Company (Chris Coleman, Artistic Director; Charles Varin, Managing Director), opening on 10 February 2023. The cast and creative contributors were:

PAUL .... Gareth Saxe
SEIF..Wasim No'mani
MAHA ....Ani Djirdjirian
JEAN .... Kate MacCluggage
BOATMAN/ MUSEUM GUARD/ DOORMAN..... James Rana

Director... Chris Coleman
Dramaturg...Nakissa Etemad
Psychodramaturgy...Barbara Hort
Set design.. Lisa M. Orzolek
Lighting design ....Robert J Aguilar
Original music and sound design............... David R Molina
Costume design....................................... Lex Liang
Dialect coach .... Louis Sallan
Intimacy choreography .... Samantha Egle
Production management.................................. Peggy Carey
Production stage manager .... Martinique M Barthel
Assistant stage manager .... Anne M Jude
Apprentice stage manger .... Lorna Stephens

ACKNOWLEDGMENTS

Sometimes certain people come into a playwrights's
life and make all the difference in their career.
For HOTTER THAN EGYPT, as mentioned in the
dedication, I am grateful to Chris Coleman and all the
people at the Denver Center who first rolled the dice
with this play in their 2020 New Play Summit. And
then rolled again when they gave it a full production in
February 2023.

And to John Langs and Nakissa Etemad, thank you for
teaming up to co-produce the world premiere of this
play at your respective theaters (ACT in Seattle, and
Marin Theatre Company). Your support has meant
everything.

And to all the actors who participated in the workshop
and productions of HOTTER THAN EGYPT: You have
taught me so much about the text, and how to better
refine it. Thank you.

And thank you to Samara Harris for being in my
corner as my agent.

And to Michael Fellmeth and Christopher Gould
at Broadway Play Publishing Inc: thank you for
championing my work over the years.

CHARACTERS

PAUL, *American from the US, late 40s to early 60s, business man.*

SEIF, *Egyptian, late 20s to mid 30s, tour guide.*

MAHA, *Egyptian, late 20s to mid 30s, former tour guide, aspiring fashion designer.*

JEAN, *American from the US, late 40s to early 60s, formerly a stay-at-home mother.*

BOATMAN/ MUSEUM GUARD/ DOORMAN, *Egyptians, any ages between 30s and 60s.*

Notes:

The BOATMAN, MUSEUM GUARD *and the* DOORMAN *are played by the same actor.*

When SEIF *and* MAHA *"speak in Arabic" (untranslated) they won't have an accent. When speaking to* PAUL *and* JEAN *in English they will have an accent.*

A slash (/) in a sentence indicates that overlap should begin at that point.

The play runs without an intermission.

AUTHOR'S NOTE

A couple of notes to the actors and director:

Maha and Seif love each other. That should not be forgotten even when Maha is being critical of Seif.

Also, in Scene 3 in particular, be careful the acrimony between Paul and Jean doesn't get too heated. Animated, yes, and certainly there's a moment when Jean lets loose, but be careful the scene doesn't descend into a shouting match. They're not *trying* to be hurtful (again, outside of a moment or two). It's just that what they're saying ends up being hurtful/ painful. These are depth charges going off underwater (for the most part), not huge and visible land explosions.

Scene 1

(Hotel room in Cairo. A map is spread out on the bed. PAUL *holds a whiskey.* SEIF *and* MAHA *have slight accents.* SEIF *more than* MAHA.*)*

PAUL: But—do you believe that sincerely? Or are you being contrary? For the sake of being contrary?

SEIF: "Contrary"? I do not know / this—

PAUL: Argumentative. For the sake of argument. Why are you smiling? Did I put my foot in it?

SEIF: I consider what you say.

PAUL: I'm genuinely curious. Has there ever been in history, and maybe there was, any kind of theocracy that worked out well.

*(*MAHA *breaks away to get the cheese platter.)*

SEIF: But is not your country a great power now?

PAUL: You mean because of the Puritans?

SEIF: They started the road for your success, no?

PAUL: It wasn't the Puritans, it was the revolution of 1776. Throwing the English out and saying "enough", we're not beholden to anybody but ourselves.

SEIF: We share this in common—

*(*PAUL, *taking a slice of cheese from the tray offered by* MAHA:*)*

PAUL: Thank you.

SEIF: —this wish.

PAUL: What wish?

(SEIF *starts to take something from the tray, but* MAHA *moves it out of reach and walks away.*)

SEIF: Saying we want to be free. We fight the British too.

PAUL: But we didn't overthrow one tyranny to bring in another. I love this cheese, by the way. What's it called?

MAHA: "Gibna Roumy".

PAUL: I'd love to find this in Wisconsin. By the way, I'm not impugning your religion. Islam has done a lot of great things — I've read.

SEIF: What is "impu—ning"?

MAHA: *(Arabic)* "Attacking".

PAUL: What was that?

MAHA: I translate the word into Arabic.

PAUL: It just seems to me politics and religion never mix well together. Ever, successfully. (*About the cheese again*) God, seriously, I love this. It's so tart. Just the right amount of sharpness.

SEIF: What I try and say before:—

MAHA: *(Aside to* SEIF *in Arabic, pasting a smile)* But do you have to say anything at all.

PAUL: *(To* MAHA*)* And what was that? What you just said.

MAHA: I say discussing religion and politics is always a good way to make friends.

PAUL: Oh don't worry about that. I can handle it.

SEIF: *(To* PAUL *and* MAHA*)* Religion *in* politics, why not?

MAHA: *(Aside to* SEIF *in Arabic, smiling)* I hate you so much right now.

SEIF: Politics is about deciding laws, how we live, no? Why not choose laws that a holy book *(Makes a stamping motion)* puts a stamp on.

MAHA: *(To* PAUL*)* Before I forget, do you want to go to the Egyptian Museum first or Khan El-Khalili?

PAUL: Either way. Whatever Jean wants.

SEIF: *(Arabic, semi-smiling)* I can discuss this with them later.

MAHA: *(Arabic, pasting a smile)* I am trying to change the subject.

SEIF: *(Arabic, semi-smiling)* I want to see how soon before he starts insulting our religion.

MAHA: *(Arabic, pasting a smile)* We don't argue with tourists, we *entertain* them.

PAUL: When you two do that, switch to Arabic, I get nervous. Like you're plotting something I shouldn't hear.

MAHA: We plot your happiness.

PAUL: *(A chuckle)* Oh, then plot away.

MAHA: More Roumy?

*(*PAUL *takes the cheese as the door opens.* JEAN *enters wearing a bikini. She has a towel wrapped around her waist and carries a small beach bag.)*

JEAN: *(To* MAHA *and* SEIF*)* Oh, hello. You're early. Weren't we meeting at four? I thought you two kept telling me how Egyptians are never on time.

PAUL: They can't make the felucca ride. They called to ask if they could come earlier.

MAHA: We're very sorry. Family from Alexandria suddenly visit for a day and we must see them.

JEAN: *(To* PAUL*)* You should have called, I'd have come up sooner. Yum, food. *(She goes to get something from the tray.)*

PAUL: I didn't think you'd stay by the pool so long.

JEAN: It feels so decadent sunbathing in the middle of winter. *(She eats.)* Our neighbors shoveling snow back home. I sent Kathy a picture of me slathered in sun screen by the pool. Now *that's* rubbing it in.

PAUL: Why don't you go get changed?

JEAN: I might go down for another swim. It's still early, isn't it? The map, dear, so we can sit down. Or shall we move to the balcony. *(She goes to fold the map, but has trouble folding it up.)*

PAUL: I'll do that. Why don't you go get changed.

JEAN: *(To* MAHA *and* SEIF*)* You must come and see our winters to appreciate how lucky you have it here.

PAUL: *(Under his breath)* Hon. I don't think that's appropriate.

JEAN: What isn't?

PAUL: *(Under his breath)* What you're wearing. I'll hold down the fort while you go get changed, yeah?

JEAN: Is this not okay?

PAUL: Did you walk through the hotel like that?

JEAN: *(To* MAHA *and* SEIF*)* Was that—not appropriate?

MAHA: You're a tourist. Of course it is okay. *(To* PAUL*)* No problem.

PAUL: Following the traditions of a country, yeah?

JEAN: I was at the pool. What am I going to wear, a coat?

PAUL: Well, the women here do wear like full-on outfits when they go swimming.

(JEAN *will move the towel from her waist to wrap around her chest.*)

MAHA: Not all women.

PAUL: I didn't see one bikini last time I was at an Egyptian beach. Not even one-piece suits.

MAHA: *(To* JEAN*)* You're a tourist, it is okay.

PAUL: Some respect shown to customs. That's all I'm saying.

JEAN: Honey. You're embarrassing me. *(To* SEIF *and* MAHA*)* I'm sorry if this offends you.

MAHA: It does not. No problem.

PAUL: Unless I'm wrong. Seif? What do you think?

JEAN: Well don't turn this into a debate, for goodness sakes. I'm not exhibit number one.

PAUL: I'm just trying to be considerate of the customs here.

JEAN: You act like I've walked in naked.

PAUL: To the locals this *is* naked.

MAHA: Mr Paul, your wife is right, she is free to do this.

JEAN: *(To* MAHA*)* Is this really naked?

MAHA: Not at all.

PAUL: Thank you for saying that but we're not exactly free to do what we want here. We're visitors.

JEAN: Would you stop treating me like I've done something terrible. I'm not going to change and I'm not going to budge.

(JEAN *takes something from the tray to eat. No one says anything. Then:*)

MAHA: How was the pool?

JEAN: *(Still hurt)* It was fun.

(Another awkward beat)

JEAN: Excuse me. *(She exits into the bathroom.)*

PAUL: *(To SEIF and MAHA)* I'll— *(Starts to follow JEAN)* I'll be right back. —I'll just be a moment. *(He exits into the bathroom.)*

SEIF: *(Arabic)* It's amazing she feels no shame walking around like that.

MAHA: *(Arabic)* Why shouldn't she dress like this in a hotel? They're on holiday.

(SEIF plucks a grape, or a piece of cheese, before MAHA moves the tray away at some point.)

MAHA: *(Arabic)* We're so backwards here.

SEIF: *(Arabic)* And until we stop being backward you shouldn't encourage her. Would I wear a gallebeya in an American city?

MAHA: *(Arabic)* If you want to take over my job then please keep your personal feelings to yourself. No politics with *any* tourist. Our job is to be welcoming, not start an argument.

SEIF: *(Arabic)* He wanted a political discussion. I gave him one. I was being friendly.

MAHA: *(Arabic)* A *discussion*, not to stand there judging him.

SEIF: *(Arabic)* You don't think he judges us?

MAHA: *(Arabic)* He respects our culture, I happen to know that.

SEIF: *(Arabic)* You do, do you? I must have missed it.

MAHA: *(Arabic)* This can't be your attitude or you'll become the *anti*-tourist guide, the opposite of welcoming: insulting.

SEIF: *(Arabic)* Which could become a thing. Instead of hiring a regular tourist guide, why not be shown around by someone who shows contempt for you. Who insults you for your country's imperialism or past colonialism. Hire us and we'll tell you why you should feel guilty if you don't already, *while* exploring Egypt. Some tourists are very politically savvy that way.

MAHA: *(Arabic)* This might amuse you and feed your ego, but it'll do nothing for us and the family we want to start.

SEIF: *(Arabic)* I want a hotel room just like this for our honeymoon.

MAHA: *(Arabic)* Did you hear me, Mr let's-start-a-political-argument?

(SEIF takes MAHA's hand, pulls her onto the bed. Arabic:)

SEIF: Let's pretend it's our room for two seconds. Come on.

MAHA: *(Trying to disengage, whispering. Arabic)* They'll come out.

SEIF: *(Arabic)* One minute.

MAHA: *(Arabic)* Are you crazy? no.

SEIF: *(Arabic)* We can dream can't we.

MAHA: *(Arabic)* We can also be caught.

(MAHA and SEIF sit on the map.)

MAHA: *(Arabic)* The map. Seif!

SEIF: *(Arabic)* One day I promise to earn enough to grant your every wish.

MAHA: *(Tries to retrieve the map. Arabic)* They'll fire you and complain to the ministry.

SEIF: *(Arabic)* Are we their servants that we should worry?

MAHA: *(Arabic)* They're paying customers, get up. *(She gets up from the bed.)*

SEIF: *(Arabic)* A kiss first.

MAHA: *(Laughing for a moment, in spite of everything. Arabic)* No.

SEIF: *(Arabic)* Live dangerously for a change, try it.

MAHA: *(Arabic)* Not here.

SEIF: *(Arabic)* You'd look great in a bikini. I can see it now.

MAHA: *(Arabic. Almost playful)* Like you'd be happy if I wore one.

SEIF: *(Arabic)* Why not? In the privacy of our own house.

MAHA: *(Arabic)* "House"? Let's earn enough money to afford a bikini first. Then maybe I can wear it just for your eyes. Move.

SEIF: *(Arabic)* Why are you in such a tense mood? You've been like this for days. What's going on?

MAHA: *(Arabic)* You're such a hypocrite.

SEIF: *(Arabic)* Because I want to have fun with my fiancé?

MAHA: *(Arabic)* And earlier. Pretending to be religious. Using religion whenever it suits you.

SEIF: *(Arabic)* I was making fun of his fears. This panic they have of our religion is too much.

MAHA: *(Arabic)* You do understand this job involves dealing with foreigners, *all the time*? Especially Westerners. If you're going to resent them for being Westerners then let me get back to my job. One of us has to be earning enough.

(Stung, SEIF gets up and goes to pour himself a whiskey.)

SEIF: *(Arabic)* I'll get us the money we need. Until then I'd appreciate it if you didn't rub my lack of funds in my face.

MAHA: *(Takes the glass or bottle away from him. Arabic)* Seif. He'll smell that on your breath. And smile when you talk with them.

SEIF: *(Arabic)* I am smiling.

MAHA: *(Arabic)* Not enough.

SEIF: *(Arabic)* What are we, performing monkeys?

MAHA: *(Arabic)* I don't know why you wanted to be a tour guide if this is your attitude.

SEIF: *(Arabic)* So you can pursue what you want. We talked about this.

(SEIF sees MAHA's still wound up.)

SEIF: *(Arabic)* We agreed on it. Seriously, what's going on?

MAHA: *(Arabic)* I'm fed up. That's what's going on.

SEIF: *(Arabic)* Who isn't? Being fed up is the air we breathe in this country. Even the rats and cockroaches are fed up: "Where is the high quality garbage we're used to", I'm sure they're saying, among themselves.

MAHA: *(Arabic)* I mean it, Seif. I'm sick of us not being able to afford anything. If—*if* you keep this job and make something of it, and if I can make something happen with my designs, maybe, just maybe we can have the life we want—even half the life we want would be amazing. Otherwise, seriously: it's too much.

SEIF: *(Arabic)* You? The great spokeswoman for "things-will-get-better"? Impossible. The President of Egypt should have you by his side in case he runs out of positive things to say. And so what if we're struggling? Poverty is in. It's all the rage these days. We're part of a fashion trend.

MAHA: *(Arabic)* "Funny" is not going to get us out of this hole.

SEIF: *(Arabic)* Another survival tool, humor.

MAHA: *(Arabic)* So is a steady income, sweetie.

SEIF: *(Arabic)* Money is better, yes, but humor is cheaper. Carry it with you wherever you go.

MAHA: *(Arabic)* Please…please don't jeopardize the one thing earning us something right now—for my sake. *Our/* sake.

SEIF: *(Arabic)* Okay, okay. I'm sorry I'm not a millionaire like these Americans. This is the problem with this job: we entertain people who rub our poverty in our faces.

MAHA: *(Arabic)* It's not their fault. They're *paying* us. They *want* to help.

(PAUL enters.)

MAHA: Mr Paul. Is Ms Jean alright?

PAUL: She's fine. She's just trying to get into her dress. All the good eating we've done here has, well, it's shrunk her clothes a little.

MAHA: The same thing happens with my clothes. They change but I don't. Very strange.

PAUL: I wouldn't worry about that: I think you've still got a ways to go before worrying about not fitting into anything.

(A moment of awkwardness. Perhaps MAHA quickly glances at SEIF before saying:)

MAHA: I'll go help her.

PAUL: She'll be fine, don't worry about it.

MAHA: I should check. *(Knocking on the bathroom door)* Ms Jean. Can I come in?

JEAN: *(Off-stage)* Yes. Come in.

(MAHA *exits into the bathroom, closing the door behind her.)*

PAUL: *(Goes to get himself a drink)* Can I get you a drink? Soda, or?

SEIF: No thank you.

PAUL: I'm sorry if, er—I don't know if it did, but. If her bikini offended you? Did it?

SEIF: You are a guest here on holiday, no problem.

PAUL: True, but: it's a fine balance between enjoying yourself and respecting the customs of a country.

SEIF: I was speaking of this with Maha. If I am in America I would not wear the long robe men wear here. It would not be your custom. And may be rude to your countrymen.

PAUL: So you *were* offended by the bikini?

SEIF: I am agreeing with you about respecting customs.

PAUL: So…you were offended?

SEIF: My English is not saying what I mean. "When in Rome".

PAUL: Ah… Still sounds like you were offended. But. *(Waves the matter away)* It all gets kind of silly when you think about it. No disrespect but we all have fleshy parts, right? And we all know which parts belong where.

SEIF: Yes. And God has also made it so these parts make a reaction. The job of these—excuse my talking like this—is to join people together. And make excitement.

PAUL: I'm not sure how exciting men's parts are, even to women.

SEIF: And because of this excitement, there are customs to politely suggest how to behave. This is part of civilization, no? Rules between men and women, so there is no misunderstanding. I hope it's okay I speak honestly.

PAUL: I'd prefer it. Getting to ask questions of my hosts about their culture: what's the point of traveling if you can't do that.

SEIF: Maha worries you think I am too aggressive.

PAUL: As long as you don't think *I'm* aggressive. I respect customs and traditions, and so my comment to Jean but, occasionally, I do like to call people on their BS.

SEIF: BS? Means "bullshit", yes?

PAUL: Or "bullcrap" in polite circles.

SEIF: I am this way too. Most Egyptians, they shovel bullshit for exercise. Every day is too hard and bullshit is escape.

PAUL: Maybe that's why it keeps circulating? Because stuff isn't faced head on?

SEIF: You don't have bullshit in your country?

PAUL: We do. That's how we elected some of the people we have now. But for the most part Americans are pretty straightforward.

SEIF: Ah. Like your action heroes in Hollywood movies. Shoot from the hip.

PAUL: Something like that.

SEIF: I think "straightforward" is for people who live with a cushion under their bottom. When you have money you say what you want. People with less money must listen. Poor people say what they think rich people want to hear, and they bite their tongue. That is how they survive.

PAUL: Just to make sure, I'm not getting the bullshit treatment from you, am I?

SEIF: One hundred per cent. *(To clarify:)* I speak my mind. Which maybe not so good.

PAUL: I find that refreshing, thank you.

SEIF: Yes? Because I'm fluent in bullshit also. English, Arabic and bullshit. And only English is my foreign language.

PAUL: Funny. I hear you're getting married.

SEIF: Maha told you?

PAUL: You'll enjoy marriage. For the most part. Tomorrow will be our twenty-sixth wedding anniversary.

SEIF: Congratulations.

PAUL: Maha is a lovely woman. One of the reasons I decided to do business in your country is that she was such a great introduction to it. She has a real talent as a tour guide. She knows the history and has a passion for telling it. That's what sold me.

SEIF: She loves Egypt.

PAUL: You prefer she stay at home? Not do this job?

SEIF: I never said this.

PAUL: She said you prefer she do something else.

SEIF: She told you this?

PAUL: It came up.

SEIF: Then you know she is also a talented dress maker. I want to give her time to follow this dream. So she open her own shop and become a fashion designer.

PAUL: Mind you I don't blame you. The way women are treated here I'd be worried myself if my wife went out alone every day.

SEIF: The women in your country don't hear rude things on the street?

PAUL: They do. But—outsider's opinion, I feel if there weren't so many Egyptian police around, all kinds of pent up stuff would be let loose.

SEIF: Of course there are rude men here with no morals, but we are not wild people.

PAUL: I didn't think that at all. Not even close. I'm just a big believer in—a big booster of personal freedoms. Which doesn't seem to be available to everyone here.

SEIF: If you mean government, yes, we have problems. But even with America, in every day life, do you not have rules? You are not free to do whatever you want.

PAUL: I'm speaking of liberty as a palpable, guaranteed,—

SEIF: *(Mispronouncing it)* "Pal-bubble"?

PAUL: Protected by laws. In the same way Maha speaks passionately about Egyptian history, our story, the American one, is all about—well it's all about this struggle for freedoms.

(Perhaps around this point PAUL goes and gets the cheese tray while speaking. He holds it out to SEIF, who will politely refuse.)

PAUL: We have a ton of hypocrisy around it, not gonna lie, but that's also part of the struggle. And I do kinda evangelize about freedom because I've never taken it for granted. Again, I hope I'm not...I don't want to offend you.

SEIF: If you will allow me not to offend you back.

PAUL: Please.

SEIF: And respectfully say you are ignorant of Egypt.

PAUL: I'm only giving you my impressions.

SEIF: This is… *(Wants to insult him, instead:)* …much to think about. Thank you for — sharing.

PAUL: *(Perhaps a laugh at his own crassness)* Let me tell you one real secret to success, Seif: mouth off as much as you need to. At the end of your life you don't get points for being silent. Say your piece and screw it if people don't like it. *(Continuing before* SEIF *can respond)* And before you say I can say that because I'm rich, I wasn't always. I worked damn hard for the money I have, *and,* I mouthed off all the way to getting it.

SEIF: I think maybe you forget the times you had to shut up to get to where you are? The real dictator all around the world is empty pockets. This makes you say and do things you don't want to.

PAUL: Which is why it makes sense to free up the other half of the work force to improve a family's income. *(Continuing before* SEIF *can interrupt)* I'm butting in, I know, but when I see talent like Maha's go to waste. There are things about my country that bug me too, so no argument about our own crap. Which is why I'm thinking of running for political office, as a matter of fact. I *do* feel passionate about our American values and women's rights happen to be at the top of my list. That's all.

SEIF: *(Not meaning it)* I am sure the women in your country will be very thankful for what you do for them.

(MAHA enters.)

SEIF: *(In Arabic)* Save me before I throw this man off the balcony.

MAHA: Your wife will be out in a moment.

PAUL: I seem to have put my foot in my mouth with your fiancé.

MAHA: *(Smiling)* That's not possible. Being on holiday you are allowed to put as many feet in your mouth as you want. No tour guide would be so unprofessional as to point out that you have said something wrong.

SEIF: *(Strained smile. Arabic)* Why did you share so much about our life? He has the nerve to lecture me about how I'm treating you.

PAUL: The thing I like about Seif is he speaks his mind. I bet we'll see a whole different side of Egypt this way.

(JEAN enters in a dress that covers most of her arms and legs. She wears a shawl around her shoulders)

PAUL: That's lovely. Very stylish. *(To MAHA and SEIF.)* It's a pity you can't come with us on the boat.

MAHA: Seif will pick you up tomorrow at nine and take you to the museum. There's still so much you haven't seen. *(To JEAN)* And this will be your first time?

JEAN: *(Trying to recover)* Yes. I can't wait. So much history.

(MAHA looks pointedly at SEIF.)

SEIF: *(To JEAN and PAUL)* It will be my pleasure to show you around.

PAUL: Right: time for a felucca and a gorgeous sunset on the Nile.

SEIF: I wish you a most pleasant time. *(Smiling, in Arabic to MAHA.)* How's that for sucking up?

MAHA: *(Smiling, in Arabic)* Shut up.

PAUL: Great. Until tomorrow then.

(Transitional lights and music)

Scene 2

(PAUL *and* JEAN *in a felucca. The* BOATMAN *is dressed in a gallebeya and headdress. The* BOATMAN *will stand, or sit behind* PAUL *and* JEAN. *Warm light from the sunset. A faint sound of water lapping that will perhaps slowly fade out)*

PAUL: Last time I did this, I imagined you sitting beside me and here you are. Can you believe it? A couple of winter birds floating on the Nile. It's hard not to be swept up by the romance of it all. Oh: *(Gets up and moves in front of her. He takes out his camera.)* I keep forgetting to take pics.

JEAN: Don't, please.

PAUL: Let's make our friends back home jealous.

JEAN: I wish you wouldn't.

PAUL: I'll get the boat guy behind you as well. *(To the* BOATMAN, *holding up his camera)* Yes?

(The BOATMAN *gives a thumbs up.)*

JEAN: Please don't. I'm not feeling well.

PAUL: *(Snapping a few photos)* You look perfect in this light. Glamor shots.

JEAN: Paul.

PAUL: One more of us together. It would be silly to waste the moment.

(As PAUL *moves to the* BOATMAN:)*

JEAN: Be careful, you'll fall over.

PAUL: *(To the* BOATMAN) Yes? Take photo?

(The BOATMAN *holds out his hand for the camera,* PAUL *gives it to him.)*

PAUL: Thanks. We're here, hon. In Egypt, for goodness sakes. And smile would you. You look like you're waiting in the dentist's office.

JEAN: I am smiling.

PAUL: A little more?

JEAN: *(Pasting it on)* Could he hurry up and take the picture.

(Nothing happens)

PAUL: *(To* BOATMAN*)* Button's right there on the—. Let me show you.

(PAUL gets up to show the BOATMAN*. The* BOATMAN *snaps a photo. The flash goes off.)*

PAUL: Okay. Well, wait until— *(He sits back down next to* JEAN*.)* Okay, now. Go ahead.

(The BOATMAN *looks through the viewfinder without taking a photo.)*

PAUL: Anytime…take the photo.

JEAN: He's just staring. He's staring at us.

PAUL: *(Standing up to go to him)* Oh for god's sake, it's right there. You press the—

(The flash goes off.)

PAUL: Good. That's the button. *(He sits back down.)* When I say "go"

(The flash goes off again. PAUL *has a God-give-me-patience moment.)*

PAUL: —when I say—go *then* take the picture.

JEAN: Let's do this later.

PAUL: One more. Ready? Go.

(Nothing)

PAUL: *Go* goddamn it.

(The BOATMAN *does not take the photo. Light change. Everyone freezes except* JEAN*. There is an accompanying high-pitched sound.)*

JEAN: I think I'm going to scream. Wait…am I screaming already? Am I screaming out loud? —Oh my god. I think I am. I'm really screaming.

(Lights back to normal. JEAN *clamps her hand over her mouth. The high pitched sound ends. Both the* BOATMAN *and* PAUL *unfreeze and look startled.)*

PAUL: What's the matter?

JEAN: What do you mean?

PAUL: What was that? What did you scream for?

JEAN: Did I?

PAUL: *Yes.*

JEAN: Oh—no.

*(*PAUL, *to the* BOATMAN, *taking the camera back:)*

PAUL: Everything's fine. It's all good, thank you. *(Sits back down next to* JEAN.*)* What the hell's wrong with you? Everything's setting you off.

JEAN: I'm sorry.

PAUL: Is this…? Are you…? *(Trying to be delicate)* I know changes are supposed to happen around this time.

JEAN: *(Knowing what he means, but looks at her watch anyway.)* You mean around four forty-five PM?

PAUL: I mean—

JEAN: This isn't menopause.

PAUL: Okay.

JEAN: And it isn't PMS. Even PMS isn't PMS. I wish people would stop with that put-down.

PAUL: *Okay.* Not so loud.

JEAN: You think he understands PMS? *(To* BOATMAN*)* Do you know what PMS means?

BOATMAN: (*Smiling, gesturing out*) Nile: beautiful.

JEAN: There. Not a clue.

PAUL: What is going on?

JEAN: I wish you hadn't embarrassed me this afternoon.

PAUL: Jean? We have all year to quarrel. It's not everyday we're on the Nile. Can we just enjoy ourselves while we're here?

JEAN: Why do you do that? Hurry past whenever I want to talk about what's upsetting me.

PAUL: I was trying to save you from embarrassment. I don't agree with this covering-up sham either, but I do know how they react here. Seeing a woman half naked. And I do go out of my way to understand your point of view, by the way.

JEAN: No you don't. —No. You don't.

PAUL: That's what *you* hurry past: acknowledging that I have and do make the effort.

JEAN: Is it such an effort to understand me?

PAUL: Let's—Jesus, let's just save this for later, okay? I'm sure you won't forget to bring it up again.

(*Beat*)

JEAN: I don't feel properly dressed now. You've made me feel so self-conscious.

PAUL: You're fine.

JEAN: I feel everyone stares at me.

PAUL: You *are* being stared at. You're a foreigner and a woman. You're the exotic thing to them.

JEAN: I didn't feel this way before you embarrassed me.

(*Beat*)

PAUL: It's kind of arrogant to think you can just be yourself without thinking about where you are. It's like walking into someone's home wearing only underwear. You *can't* just be yourself here.

JEAN: It was a swimsuit.

PAUL: It's called being culturally sensitive.

JEAN: This isn't a class assignment, it's a vacation.

PAUL: It would be if you stopped overreacting to everything…. I really think you should check in with your doctor when we get home. This could be a simple—adjustment to your meds.

(Slight beat)

JEAN: I'd like to go back now.

PAUL: Please don't ruin this. *Please.* This is supposed to be relaxing. *(Slight beat) You* wanted to come with me on this trip. We have the Nile. The sunset. We even have the picturesque local guy steering the boat.

(PAUL waves at the BOATMAN who smiles and waves back.)

PAUL: Let's at least enjoy ourselves. It cost a bunch, why waste it?

JEAN: *(Slight beat, quiet)* I'm just worried I'm going to scream again.

(The sound of the lapping fades back in and quickly increases in volume. During which there's silence between JEAN and PAUL. He looks increasingly pissed off. Then:)

PAUL: *(To the BOATMAN, gesturing)* We're going back. Please turn the boat around. We're going back.

(Transitional lights and music. The shift should be quick.)

Scene 3

(Hotel room. PAUL *starts taking off his clothes. He will get into his pajamas.)*

PAUL: *(Perhaps starts off-stage in the bathroom)* I can't believe you did that. *(Comes out with his pajamas)* Ruined it. And why? Because I stopped you from making a fool of yourself? So next time I see a bit of food on your mouth, or you get someone's name wrong, or any number of things I should just ignore that?

JEAN: Why are you getting ready for bed? It's early.

PAUL: Yes, it is. We could be exploring a whole new part of the world, but because you're suddenly too self-conscious and feel everyone's staring at you...

JEAN: I don't think that. I never said that.

PAUL: I'm serious, Jean: make an appointment with your doctor, because I don't know how to help you anymore.

JEAN: Don't make me out to be some crazy person because I didn't like what you said.

PAUL: You cried out in the boat for no reason.

JEAN: Of course there's a reason. There's always a reason.

PAUL: Then tell me what it is so I can help you.

*(*JEAN *considers how to reply.)*

PAUL: You know what, never mind. Let's just go to bed and get an early start on the museum.

JEAN: I may want to go out later.

PAUL: Tonight?

JEAN: Yes, tonight.

PAUL: Alone?

JEAN: If you don't want to come.

PAUL: I wouldn't advise that.

JEAN: Why not?

PAUL: You'll freak out when all the men start staring at you.

JEAN: I was fine by the pool, it's you who made me feel ashamed.

PAUL: Okay, we're not—I'm not going over that again. If you want to go out and endanger yourself go ahead. *(Silence as he continues changing into his pajamas. Whenever he's finished, he'll get a drink from the mini-fridge.)*

JEAN: *(Half to herself, quiet)* The real problem is you've stopped wanting me.

PAUL: What?

JEAN: You don't. Not really. Not anymore.

PAUL: What are you talking about?

JEAN: You've stopped wanting me. Physically.

(PAUL stares at JEAN.)

JEAN: It's true.

PAUL: What do you think I was trying to do on the boat?

JEAN: The motions, yes, you go through the motions.

PAUL: You're the one who recoils from me. I can feel you rolling your eyes whenever I start. "Here he goes again, time to check out."

JEAN: I've never felt that.

PAUL: You have many fine qualities, but a healthy sex drive is not one of them.

JEAN: I've never "recoiled".

PAUL: Not physically, but I feel it.

JEAN: That's not true.

PAUL: Arctic winds. The temperature in the room actually drops when I approach you. Now you feel *I'm* cold towards you?

JEAN: I don't know who you're talking about. I've always reciprocated.

PAUL: Maybe in a subtle, spiritual way. So subtle I don't feel it. But that's fine. Couples settle down into a comfortable routine, I get it. There's only so many times you can look at each other before, you know— you stop checking each other out—in that way. I know *I'm* not much to look at these days.

JEAN: *(Considers the implications of what he just said.)* Are you saying *I'm* not much to look at these days?

PAUL: Would you stop always making this about yourself.

JEAN: Who else are you referring to?

PAUL: I'm speaking in general, couples in general, they start to—the spark—it fizzles out. A little bit. Entropy happens to everything.

JEAN: "Entropy"? That's pretty drastic when you start dragging in the laws of physics to describe a rough spot in a marriage. I've never stopped finding you attractive.

PAUL: Oh come on. We're past lying to each other.

JEAN: I still find you attractive. When you're not being so annoying that I can't look at you.

PAUL: I was the one trying to be romantic on the boat.

JEAN: You can't suddenly turn it on when that spigot's been dry for months. Years it feels like, and then expect me to know it's happening and respond.

PAUL: It's the *Nile*, at *sunset*, on a *boat*. If that's not a postcard romantic moment I don't know what is.

(Slight beat)

JEAN: If only it didn't feel slightly condescending when you touched me. Like you're being charitable towards someone you don't want to be with anymore.

PAUL: What?

JEAN: "Let me put in my two cents as a husband and give her some attention so I don't have to bother again for awhile."

PAUL: I'm—genuinely shocked you think that. Two people can be this close and live in alternate universes.

JEAN: When was the last time we made love?

PAUL: That's why we're on vacation. So we can rekindle. That's the whole point.

JEAN: I don't feel rekindled.

PAUL: That's because you're stubbornly ignoring my romantic gestures.

JEAN: I must keep missing them. I guess I'm not the only one being subtle.

PAUL: Would you prefer I throw you on the bed and have at you.

JEAN: Wonderful, yes. Consider me thrown. In fact... *(She jumps on the bed, splaying her limbs.)*

PAUL: What are you doing?

JEAN: Well I'm not airing myself because the weather is balmy.

PAUL: And that's supposed to be a turn on?

JEAN: With some couples it might be considered that, yes. Voilà: romantic gesture.

(PAUL goes to refill his glass. Beat)

JEAN: I was reading in Islam that if a man fails to satisfy his wife sexually that's grounds for divorce. What do you think of that? The woman has the right to leave. I think they're onto something…. Would you ever tell me if you were seeing someone else?

(PAUL *doesn't respond. Which suddenly makes it an actual question.*)

JEAN: Are you?

PAUL: *(Hesitates)* No.

JEAN: Hold on. Hold on. Are you?

PAUL: Talking with you lately—

JEAN: Paul?

PAUL: You get emotional for no reason. I don't know if you think it'll force me to open up or what?

JEAN: You *are* seeing someone?

PAUL: Oh God, I want to say yes just to throw it in your face.

JEAN: So it is "yes"?

PAUL: It's called being mature enough to understand that any marriage goes through phases. And if we've slowed down in one area it's because we're exploring other—equally important areas of our marriage. It's so strange to have you be the one to complain about this.

(*Taking note of* JEAN's *look:*)

PAUL: What? —It's times like these *I* want to scream.

JEAN: Just tell me if you've met someone else.

PAUL: Why isn't the life we have enough?

JEAN: Because I don't know what that is anymore.

(*Beat. Then:*)

PAUL: I love you.

JEAN: Oh, crap. That sounds ominous.

PAUL: I do. But…sure. As will happen, often, it's not uncommon… that, yes—I…I don't find you as…in that way. —I can't fake that. If you're all hell-bent on "let's be honest".

(Slight beat)

JEAN: But you can fake loving me? You can go through those motions?

PAUL: I'm not faking that. I genuinely have feelings for you.

JEAN: You might as well pat me on the shoulder and say "There, there, you're not a total write-off, I still feel *something* for you."

PAUL: I don't even have the energy to correct that.

JEAN: Can I ask when things changed for you?

PAUL: Why can't you accept that things *do* change? Getting older brings its own set of wonderful things. *(Perhaps he goes to refill his drink again.)*

JEAN: Am I too old for you now? Is that it? …Am I?

PAUL: *(Not very convincing)* No.

JEAN: If you want to give me the perfect anniversary present, honesty would be terrific. And a drink. To help it go down.

(PAUL will pour JEAN a drink and hand it to her at some point as the conversation continues.)

PAUL: It's unrealistic to expect any couple, frankly, to expect them to see each other in the same way they did when they first met. We aren't the same people. *I* haven't aged any better. I don't preen in front of the mirror the way I used to, and you know how much I used to love to do that.

JEAN: So…

PAUL: I knew you couldn't handle it. You say you want honesty but not really.

JEAN: So—what bit the dust for you first? My face? My boobs?

PAUL: I'm not doing this.

JEAN: We'll end up hating each other if we keep pretending. Maybe we can stay good friends at least.

PAUL: At least?

JEAN: If you find me unattractive, what would/ be the point?

PAUL: I don't. I don't find/ you unattractive.

JEAN: If you've lost interest in me,—

PAUL: You're a gorgeous woman.

JEAN: Paul.

PAUL: We should have stayed home if we're going to do this.

JEAN: You've lost interest in me sexually. That's what you're saying. Yes?

(Beat. PAUL *feels trapped. Then he nods.)*

JEAN: There. That wasn't so difficult.

PAUL: It's my problem for not seeing what's in front of me.

JEAN: I'm not what I used to be, I agree.

PAUL: Neither am I, so what?

JEAN: But I *was* gorgeous. Wasn't I? When we met.

PAUL: Oh my god. A knockout.

JEAN: I held my own.

PAUL: You did more than that. I bragged about you. With friends.

JEAN: Did you? You never told me.

PAUL: It's embarrassing how much. I'm sorry for objectifying you.

JEAN: It sounds thrilling. Tell me.

PAUL: Oh—you know—what guys say when they see someone hot.

JEAN: I was hot.

PAUL: Very. Hotter than Egypt.

(JEAN *and* PAUL *look at each other. He leans in to kiss her, but before he can:*)

JEAN: But not so much now.

PAUL: What about me? Look at this. Look at this flab.

JEAN: It's not the same thing with a guy.

PAUL: *(Lifts up pajama top and grabs a side of his waist.)* What's this?

JEAN: A guy ages like cracked leather. Distinguished.

PAUL: There is no such thing as distinguished flab. A little gray on the side is distinguished. This is beer and bad metabolism. And gravity.

JEAN: *(Lifting up her cheeks) This* is gravity.

PAUL: Have you seen my ass lately? I didn't know anything could drop so fast.

JEAN: I haven't seen your ass in a while, no.

(PAUL *draws near* JEAN *again.*)

PAUL: Well—let me reintroduce you. I can't promise you'll like what you see. Prepare yourself.

(PAUL *leans in, he kisses* JEAN. *He notes her lack of enthusiasm. Or perhaps she just turns her head again when he tries to kiss her.*)

PAUL: You complain…then shut down when I do something.

JEAN: Who is she?

(PAUL *doesn't answer.*)

JEAN: Secrets are such strange things with married couples, aren't they? One really big one comes along after so many years of marriage and you feel it actually abduct the person you've loved. You can ignore it like I've done. But eventually you notice the person you've been with for so long isn't really there anymore.

PAUL: Yes.

(*Slight beat*)

JEAN: "Yes" to what I just said? Or...you are seeing someone?

PAUL: I'm seeing someone.

(*Slight beat*)

JEAN: Do I know her?

PAUL: (*Hesitates*) Yes.

(*Slight beat*)

JEAN: Who is she?

(PAUL *doesn't answer.*)

JEAN: Who? —Kathy? —Is it Kathy? She's always had more than a work-buddy vibe. Her flirting is so obvious you could grease a rusty hinge with it.

PAUL: Do you really want me to tell you or not?

JEAN: Well don't make me feel like I'm reneging on some promise by reacting. I'm sorry for not being as open minded as I thought I would be to hearing my husband is fucking another woman.

PAUL: I should have followed my instincts and kept my mouth shut. And it hasn't come to that yet.

JEAN: Oh goody, you're just circling the drain. Who is she?

PAUL: I can't believe we've flown thousands of miles to do this.

JEAN: You have the *nerve* to plan our anniversary while having an affair?

PAUL: You're the one who insisted we combine our anniversary with my business trip.

JEAN: And how dare you tell me I'm not hot anymore.

PAUL: I never said that.

JEAN: I may not be all that I was but I can still get laid.

PAUL: I'm sure you can.

JEAN: I could walk out that door and find a guy in five minutes.

PAUL: I don't think that's something to brag about.

JEAN: Fuck you! …I can't believe I've been acting the way I have all this time, tip-toeing around your moods. Wondering how *I* could change, or make myself more attractive. The hundred, *hundreds* of anti-aging products I've drowned my face in. Those fucking aerobics classes and spin fucking cycles. Making me feel it was *my* problem to solve. How young is she? Twelve? Twenty-three? She can't be over thirty, that would be past the expiration date for you.

PAUL: "Let's be honest", you said.

JEAN: That's before I knew what you were going to be honest about.

PAUL: I'm trying to show you some respect by telling you.

JEAN: You lie to me for months, years? and now you want to get points for two seconds of honesty?

PAUL: It hasn't been years.

JEAN: How long? Has she been the only one?

PAUL: I'm glad you forced this. I thought we could muddle along but maybe we can't. And the way you parade your suffering in that passive aggressive way of yours, like you're some martyr. Waiting to be declared a saint for what? Apart from the affair I've been a great husband.

JEAN: You mean apart from the assassination how was the play Mrs Lincoln?

PAUL: I've treated you well. We've had, we *are* having good times.

JEAN: While you've been cheating on me.

PAUL: Recently. It's only been a minute, and like I said we haven't actually done anything yet.

JEAN: Who is she?

PAUL: You're... (*Hesitates*) ...you're not going to like it. Look, this can't be the way we end things, not after a life time together. I won't contest anything. If you want the house, it's yours.

JEAN: We're getting a divorce already? We haven't even finished discussing the reasons for getting one.

PAUL: You deserve, you do, so much more. We can both, we both get to start over. We *haven't* been happy, I agree, and like you said, we can at least stay friends.

JEAN: Oh—gag.

PAUL: It takes two to break up a marriage, you know.

JEAN: Yes, one of them gets old and the other one chucks her.

PAUL: It's Maha.

(*It takes a moment for the name to register.*)

JEAN: Who?

PAUL: Maha. —From this afternoon? She was my tour guide on my last trip. That's how we…met, and… clicked.

JEAN: Maha?

(PAUL *nods.*)

JEAN: Who's engaged to be married?

PAUL: I don't know how keen she is about that.

JEAN: Maha who's *actually* twelve?

PAUL: She's thirty two. (*Age can be adjusted within the age-range specified.*)

JEAN: Next to you, twelve.

PAUL: We get along. We like each other, a lot. She's… she's shown feelings towards me. She dreams of leaving Egypt. Starting over somewhere else.

JEAN: *That's* why she likes you. She wants to get to the States.

PAUL: No. We've discussed that. There's a real connection. Maybe I'm fooling myself but I don't think so.

JEAN: Wait: you've discussed running away together already?

PAUL: In a round-about way. She doesn't think it can happen, or that I'm serious, but, why not?

JEAN: Paul…I say this not because you've just finished crushing me, but the only reason a good looking girl like her would fall for a man your age is if she sees you as a way out. You may be "distinguished", but you're also a little dumpy. I like dumpy. In an old comfy chair kind of way. But I'm not sure that's why she's drawn to you.

(PAUL *starts dressing. He will also take his suitcase and hurriedly throw in some clothes.*)

PAUL: You're right. Someone my age. How stupid can I be. I don't want to believe it myself. I go from hoping, to thinking I'm nuts. But we've been—we've corresponded. Months now. And phone calls. She's poured her heart out to me. It's more than an infatuation. I think we genuinely—and maybe it's too early to say I love her, but I think I could.

JEAN: *(Wondering what he's doing)* Paul?

PAUL: And she wants to get to know me more.

JEAN: Paul, what—?

PAUL: *(Overlapping)* Imagine: someone wants to get to know me deeply again at my age. When was the last time you looked at me like you were fascinated by anything I had to say?

JEAN: What are you doing? Where are you going?

PAUL: Well there's no point going on as we are, is there? Look: whatever you want. I'm not going to fight you. I still love you. All these years together, they have to add up to something. I don't understand couples who spend a life time together and then end up hating each other. *(He sees something in the pocket of his suitcase and retrieves it.)* Oh, here's…when I snuck away yesterday, I got you—for your—anniversary present. *(Holds out a small jewelry box)* Maha helped to—.

(PAUL thinks better than to say she helped pick it. He hands JEAN the package, or, if she doesn't take it, he places it on the bed, or on another nearby surface.)

PAUL: I'll check into another hotel. Everything's paid for so you might as well finish the whole Egypt tour. I'll try and move most of my things out of the house by the time you come back. *(Suitcase in hand)* I…I think this was meant to happen. I honestly think we'll laugh about this one day.

(PAUL looks at JEAN, perhaps expecting some response.)

PAUL: Okay…well… Bye.

(PAUL *exits.* JEAN *stands there. Slight beat. Transitional lights and music*)

Scene 4

(*The Egyptian Museum. If possible, the statue of Khafre is brought on. The spectacle of the statue appearing would be dramatically useful at this moment. Or, the statue can just be referenced as an off-stage piece. Or perhaps we just see the shadow of the statue.* JEAN *and* SEIF *are present. A* MUSEUM GUARD *will enter and listen to* SEIF.)

SEIF: And here is the statue of the pharaoh Khafre. He build the second tallest pyramid in Giza. Also the mysterious Sphinx. The sphinx is part of Egyptian and Greek mythology but it starts here in Egypt. You may know the riddle of the sphinx? What walks on four legs in the morning, two in the afternoon and three in the evening? Or the riddle of the two sisters: one sister gives birth to the other, and the other sister in turn gives birth to the first. Who are they? And if you didn't get it right: (*He makes a gobbling motion with his mouth and hands.*) The sphinx eats you for being stupid. The right answer is the sisters are night and day. Day gives birth to night and night gets pregnant with day and so on. And you know the famous answer to the first riddle.

(JEAN *looks like she's in a state of shock. Slight beat. She realizes she's being asked a question.*)

JEAN: (*Perhaps thinking of* PAUL) Man.

SEIF: Correct. Though the real riddle is why put up with these silly riddles? The pharaoh and his priests keep you busy with stupid stories. They don't want you to ask the tough questions like why are you breaking your back for the pharaoh?

(Noticing that the MUSEUM GUARD *is paying too close attention.)*

SEIF: Better you ask this pharaoh a riddle yourself like: what is asleep in the morning, rises up in the afternoon, and starts dreaming when finally awake at night?

*(*JEAN *again realizes she is being asked a question.)*

JEAN: What?

SEIF: The people. *(To the* MUSEUM GUARD. *Arabic)* Can I help you?

MUSEUM GUARD: *(Arabic)* What kind of lecture is this?

SEIF: *(Arabic)* Why is it your business? Isn't the museum busy enough today that you should follow us?

MUSEUM GUARD: *(Arabic)* You're saying bad things about our history.

SEIF: *(Arabic)* I'm still trying to understand why you're speaking to me. *(To* JEAN*)* Let us go to the next exhibit.

MUSEUM GUARD: *(Arabic)* If you're with the protesters outside, bringing your demonstrations in here, then I must ask you to leave.

JEAN: Is something the matter?

MUSEUM GUARD: *(Accent, to* JEAN*)* No protest here.

SEIF: *(Arabic)* God give me patience: does she look like she's dressed for a protest?

MUSEUM GUARD: *(Arabic)* I don't know how foreigners dress for a protest. Maybe this is how.

SEIF: *(To* JEAN*)* Is it the fashion in your country to come to a protest well dressed?

JEAN: Am I not dressed properly?

MUSEUM GUARD: *(Arabic)* We don't want troublemakers. If she is one of those foreigners who come to Egypt to cause trouble, she can leave now.

SEIF: *(Arabic)* Listen to me, if you don't get out of my face I'm going to find your supervisor and wipe the floor with you.

MUSEUM GUARD: *(Arabic)* I will bring him here myself so he can hear how you're slandering our country. *(He exits.)*

SEIF: *(Partially follows the* MUSEUM GUARD *as he exits. Arabic)* Yes, I am here to protest! I'm here to protest your stupid mind and every small thought you've ever had that pollutes our country! Go! Tell your supervisor there's a tourist and a tour guide starting a revolution in a museum! *(Slight beat)* Sometimes this country makes me want to smash something.

JEAN: Was that my fault?

SEIF: No.

JEAN: Is it what I'm wearing?

SEIF: Not you, it is this man. He thinks we are something to do with those idiot protesters outside. Put a little man in a uniform and suddenly he wants to tell you what to do.

JEAN: I made such an effort to read up on your country. I wanted to make sure I didn't offend anyone.

SEIF: It is not you, Ms Jean, please: do not spend any thought on this.

JEAN: Maybe my husband is right: I am clueless, and old. The me in my head clearly has no idea how I'm coming across.

SEIF: No problem. Your clothes are very elegant. And the men staring at you are not doing this because you are old, believe me.

(JEAN *looks around.*)

JEAN: Men are staring?

SEIF: I say this to inform you that you are not old.

JEAN: You don't think I'm old?

SEIF: *(Pointing to the statue) This* is old. Everything in this museum is old. Next to them you are a spring chicken.

JEAN: Next to them my grandmother is a spring chicken. *(Then:)* My husband is going out with your fiancé.

SEIF: Yes. She told me. They are going to meet Mr Shafeek early about your husband's business. —What is it? I hope this stupid man has not upset you.

JEAN: No. It's just…I've been crying out recently for no reason. And I think I'm about to do it again.

SEIF: "Crying out"? How do you mean?

JEAN: This may be loud.

(Spotlight on JEAN. SEIF *freezes.* JEAN's *body tenses up as we hear that piercing high-pitched sound heard earlier in Scene 2. Then, normal lighting resumes and the sound fades out quickly. Seif unfreezes. The* MUSEUM GUARD *rushes on.)*

MUSEUM GUARD: *(Arabic)* What happened?

SEIF: *(To* JEAN*)* Ms Jean. Are you okay?

MUSEUM GUARD: *(Arabic)* Are you or are you not organizing a protest in here?

SEIF: *(Arabic)* We have nothing to do with them!

JEAN: Can we get out of here?

SEIF: Yes, let's go.

*(*SEIF *and* JEAN *exit.)*

(As they exit. Arabic:)

MUSEUM GUARD: I'm notifying the museum. You'll be barred from stepping foot in this or any museum ever again. You've no business speaking about our great history to anyone. Shame on you!

(Music and light change as we transition to:)

Scene 5

(The street. Sounds of cars and of protests)

SEIF: This way we can't go. The protests are coming from there. We must go around Tahrir Square.

JEAN: I don't want to go back to the hotel.

SEIF: We call your husband.

JEAN: No. Can we go somewhere quiet. Away from people. Your place?

SEIF: My room is not for receiving guests. It is very small.

JEAN: I don't care. I like small. Small is cute.

SEIF: This kind of small is not cute. Even the mice are looking for a bigger place.

JEAN: I can't go back to the hotel. Please.

SEIF: Do you know other people in Cairo?

(Seeing JEAN doesn't)

SEIF: Alright. Alright. We go this way.

(JEAN and SEIF exit. Sounds of the protest increase. Transitional music and lights to:)

Scene 6

(SEIF's *room consists of a bed, an uncomfortable chair, and a tiny kitchen—more a hot plate situation, perhaps. The space looks pretty miserable and threadbare. The protest sounds fade out as* SEIF *and* JEAN *enter the area. He immediately tidies up the bed.)*

SEIF: I am embarrassed to invite you. It is not my place. It is my cousin's. He works in the Gulf now. Please: *(Gestures towards the bed, but realizes it is inappropriate.)* Or: *(Gestures towards the chair, as he clears it of whatever's on it.)* You have choice. This ugly chair, or, half-way out the window, or...

JEAN: The bed is fine. It's perfect.

SEIF: *(He attempts to tidy up the space a little more.)* This room is like a sweaty armpit. If you are small bacteria, this room is perfect. If you are human, it is an armpit.

JEAN: It suits my mood perfectly.

SEIF: Your mood must be very bad.

JEAN: I mean it's cozy.

SEIF: My fiancée already says I am bad at this tourist thing. If she sees you are upset, she will say it is my fault and tell me to give up my job.

JEAN: I promise to give you glowing reviews. If I ever see her again.

SEIF: *(Takes out his cell phone)* I call her now. Tell them we're here. Can I get you something to drink? Tea?/ Coffee?

JEAN: No thank you, please don't call her.

SEIF: So they know, or your husband will worry.

(A knock on the door)

SEIF: Excuse me.

(SEIF *opens the door to the DOORMAN. He is dressed in a gallebeya and a skullcap. He carries a letter in his hand.* SEIF *does not open the door all the way.*)

SEIF: What?

DOORMAN: *(Arabic)* Ms Maha left this for you this morning.

SEIF: *(Takes the letter. Arabic)* Thanks, bye.

(*Seeing Jean, the Doorman takes a few steps into the apartment.*)

SEIF: *(Arabic)* Where do you think you're going?

DOORMAN: And who do we have here?

SEIF: *(Blocking him. Arabic)* None of your business.

DOORMAN: *(Arabic)* If you're bringing women to this respectable building it is my business.

SEIF: *(Arabic)* Respectable for who? Rats? Why don't you keep this building clean instead of being so nosey.

(SEIF *half guides, half pushes the DOORMAN out of the apartment.*)

DOORMAN: *(Arabic)* I won't tell Ms Maha you have a bit on the side, I just want to see.

SEIF: *(Arabic)* Move, move, before I shove you out.

DOORMAN: *(Arabic)* Mr Seif: we have religious people in this building. You can't bring women up here, I'll tell them.

SEIF: *(Arabic)* Shout it from the roof tops if you want, but get out of my face. *(He closes the door.)*

JEAN: What was that about?

SEIF: Nothing. —There is one exhibit I didn't show you. My fellow countrymen. We are very nice, very polite people, but we are also very nosey. Everyone watches everyone. Who needs a dictator when we have each other. He thinks I bring you up here for rude things. A man and a woman who only want to talk does not make sense to him.

JEAN: People everywhere are nosey.

SEIF: And if I bring a woman here for something else so what? What business is it of his?

JEAN: You *are* engaged.

SEIF: And? This is between my fiancé and me. And God. It is a sickness this being in people's business. I love my country but sometimes I want to scream too.

(JEAN *looks a little embarrassed by* SEIF's *reminder.*)

JEAN: Yes…about that.

SEIF: Do not think of this. The question is not why you scream but why we are not *all* screaming all the time. *(Then:)* Is it something I do that upset you?

JEAN: *No.* You've been very kind. I'm just…not in a good place at the moment.

SEIF: You mean my country?

JEAN: Emotionally. Egypt I love. My husband and I… *(Considers continuing, then:)* I don't want to bore you.

SEIF: Nothing about you is boring, Ms Jean.

JEAN: Other people's problems are a little like dreams, aren't they? Fascinating only to the people who insist on telling you all about them.

SEIF: Things will become better, Inshallah. God is merciful and you are good people.

JEAN: Thank you for saying that.

SEIF: You have a good life. You travel, you see the world.

JEAN: Oh, you mean money?

SEIF: I mean life is good for you, Alhamdulillah. You live in a good country. You have children, a house, a car?

JEAN: Privileged. Sure. I should be more grateful. Do you resent us for that, by the way? American tourists? Tourists in general?

SEIF: Of course not. I love tourists. They help me take a break from Egyptians.

JEAN: Well I might if I was you—be resentful. Tourists wander through countries so oblivious of the lives of the people living there. It's so backwards when you think about it. Being shown the dead things of a country. Treating the locals as something to move aside so we can gawk at all the things long dead.

(*Perhaps* SEIF *goes and prepares Turkish coffee. He may not get around to finishing it if distracted by what* JEAN's *saying. If he does finish, he'll offer it to her.*)

SEIF: No problem with this. We are proud of our dead things.

JEAN: Your monuments *are* impressive, I have to say.

SEIF: Egypt is a gift of the Nile, but it lives because of tourists like you. You are most welcome.

JEAN: Welcomed, sure, but…I know it sounds silly— typically self-obsessive in a Western kind of way, but… liked? Do you like us?

SEIF: I have never been asked this question before. — Yes.

JEAN: Totally neurotic thing to ask. I don't usually feel so… vulnerable. Or guilty.

SEIF: Guilty?

JEAN: Wrong word perhaps. Awkward?

SEIF: You are speaking of colonialism? The history of the Western powers in this region? I was speaking of this with Maha yesterday. I did not think you'd be interested in this kind of history.

JEAN: I was thinking more on a personal level. Throwing our money around without thinking what we're doing, or how we're coming across.

SEIF: Oh. We like this part. Please: keep throwing your money around.

JEAN: I mean not really caring. Caring, yes, but not really noticing what's around us. I mean here I am in a local's apartment. This alone is a revelation. *Now* I feel I'm seeing something about Egypt. Just as fascinating as going to see a statue of Ramses, for my money. I mean, what is this?

SEIF: A coffee pot. "Kanaka".

JEAN: That's amazing. You won't find this kind of design in Wisconsin.

SEIF: You make Turkish coffee with this.

JEAN: Well there you go. I did not know that.

SEIF: You want it? Please take it.

JEAN: And this?

SEIF: It's writing. Arabic.

JEAN: It's beautiful. What's it say?

SEIF: Allah.

JEAN: And look at this design.

SEIF: This is a carpet. Very common carpet.

JEAN: I've always wanted to carpet my whole house with these kinds of patterns. We have the typical beige carpeting that kills the soul. Literally. Over the years I've felt my soul merge with that beige color and become this thing that others just...step on without bothering to wipe their shoes even. I've been meaning to rip it out for years.

SEIF: I can show you where you buy this if you want.

JEAN: The space may be small, but just—the ordinary stuff, that's what gives it character.

(SEIF *looks around the apartment.*)

SEIF: Maybe I should make this place a stop on my Cairo tour.

JEAN: Not as silly as it sounds. You can skim right through a country without once experiencing anything remotely intimate about the people who live there. This is like a real introduction. I feel like I'm finally in Egypt now. Not in a hotel room, or a museum. Or standing before a grand monument. This. (*She gestures around the room.*)

SEIF: Please ignore this Egypt. It is not our best face.

JEAN: I love this face.

SEIF: Nobody in Egypt would be proud of this. We are better.

JEAN: And I don't want to sound like some tourist who wants to slum it. Or be shown the grittier side of some place because that's supposed to be more authentic or something. I know that's a thing and that's not what I'm saying.

SEIF: I would not say this is a slum.

JEAN: Oh God no. That's not what I meant.

SEIF: There are more slummy. This is upscale slum. The high end.

JEAN: I love it. Is what I'm saying.

SEIF: And what does it matter if we like you or not? Who are we that you should care? If I had money I would say, "Here's my money, please give me good service and show me your country."

JEAN: You'd never put up with anyone that rude.

SEIF: If the guide can not keep how he feel to himself, maybe he should find other work.

JEAN: Then—wait: you're *not* sharing your true feelings with me?

SEIF: Why is this so important? What my feelings are. You should care only if I am doing my job.

JEAN: Right. Right, I'm a job.

SEIF: What I do is a job. You: you are a pleasure.

JEAN: "A pleasure". That is an upgrade.

SEIF: Showing you around gives me pleasure, yes.

JEAN: You're just being polite.

SEIF: You may not have noticed, but it is very difficult for me to be polite. Your company *is* a pleasure.

JEAN: (*Light hearted*) Prove it then.

SEIF: I would be delighted. How? More than saying this is so.

JEAN: I don't know. Kiss me? —Just for the hell of it?

SEIF: (*Awkward laugh, perhaps*) More than money I hope to earn, the different humor tourists bring, I will learn much about other countries from this I think.

JEAN: I'm quite serious. Unless you find me hideous.

SEIF: "Hideous"?

JEAN: Unattractive.

SEIF: Madame. (*Walks over to her, takes her hand and politely kisses it.*) You see. A pleasure.

JEAN: You would say that, I'm your employer. I was hoping you would kiss me on the lips. *(Less confident)* I dare you.

(Beat)

SEIF: I...

(SEIF looks increasingly uncomfortable. JEAN: expectant, nervous. Then:)

JEAN: There: more tourist humor. I had you for a second. You looked so afraid.

SEIF: I—

JEAN: The thing with humor it doesn't always translate. I mean do you even have chicken-crossing-the-road jokes here?

SEIF: A chicken crossed the road? What happened?

JEAN: Exactly, it doesn't translate. So with that kissing joke.

SEIF: A chicken crossing the road in Cairo would die. For sure.

JEAN: Crossing the road here *is* dangerous. What's up with that?

SEIF: I will have to listen better for this humor.

JEAN: So...yeah: a joke. The kissing thing. I'd never put you in such an uncomfortable position. Unless you wanted to be put in such a position. In which case I would regard it as a further extension of this more— intimate tour of Cairo?

(Slight beat. Then JEAN laughs to preempt any awkwardness. SEIF looks uncomfortable again.)

JEAN: Listen to me, I'll be doing stand-up next. *(Changing the subject)* I heard the doorman say "Maha" when he gave you that letter.

SEIF: *(Regaining his composure)* I forgot to call her.

JEAN: Don't. Just yet.

SEIF: *(Picks up the envelope)* Yesterday she said she would... *(Still trying to digest what just happened)* write down important things to remind me how to be a better tour guide.

JEAN: Oh? Can you read it to me?

SEIF: *(Opening the envelope)* I will tell you what she says if you promise not to tell her I lost my temper in the museum.

JEAN: Cross my heart.

SEIF: Maybe my fiancé will also have advice about how to be a better host. *(He unfolds the letter to read.)*

JEAN: Wait. *(She grabs the letter out of his hand.)* Let's just...take a breather. *(She places the letter on the bed. Slight beat.)* Aren't you ever curious about the lives of the people you show around? Oh, that's right, I'm officially your first tourist. Well I'd be curious.

SEIF: I am interested, of course.

JEAN: I don't know why your opinion of me matters so much. Or why I'm always feeling like I'm wearing practically nothing at all in this country. I'm so clueless most of the time. Except that can't be an excuse anymore, can it? You can't be ignorant of other people's cultures anymore. Not when it can be so hurtful. You have to make the effort to find out. You poor thing listening to me, I'm so sorry.

SEIF: No. Whatever you want. You have...

JEAN: I've paid for your time. Is that what you were going to say?

SEIF: Something is upsetting you. I would like to help.

JEAN: It's just that...it seems so strange lately not being able to grab onto anything that can...grab me back. So to speak. Ghosts. It feels like. My life, crowded with them. And not the dead kind either, living, breathing ones. Like I'm passing through lives. And people are passing through mine without once…without any kind of—contact whatsoever. It should be so basic, sharing ourselves with each other. Why is that so hard?

SEIF: *(Not understanding)* I—think I understand.

JEAN: And I'm *not* privileged. I know I check a lot of those boxes, but you have me completely wrong. Money, yes, if you don't have it it's everything. But it can't make up for wasting a life. I have a lovely house, two kids in college, if you look at the highlights of my life, "woohoo". Even "wow". And I'm the one who chose to be a stay-at-home mom. Raise my kids, create a home. I wish I could see it as an accomplishment. But my children turned out to be complete shits. The most ungrateful, spoiled—brats. I love them dearly but most days I'm thrilled they're gone. I can't wait for them to make up an excuse to skip Thanksgiving. *And* Christmas. I'll pretend to be sad, naturally, I'll make them feel a little guilty as a normal parent should. But this is my time now. And now that I can look back I think:…what a waste. *(As if the realization is hitting her only now)* The things I denied myself out of some stupid obligation to my family. The shame I'd feel at the thought of embarrassing them with *my* needs, as if *my* needs would be an interruption to their great life goals. Stuffing myself into this small, wasted hole of a life. And now I'm just…I'm done. What in my small world could I possibly do that would be so fucking embarrassing? Except this. Not living at all.

SEIF: Ms Jean…please, tell me how I can help.

JEAN: Look at you. You're so sweet listening to me.

SEIF: I want to listen.

JEAN: But that's why I'm trying to seduce you, you see. I'm sorry to put you in such an awkward position. But

that would be a good, first, healthy step for me. I know
I won't succeed so don't panic. Plus I know I'm not as
attractive as Maha.

SEIF: Ms Jean: do not say such things.

JEAN: Don't take anything I'm saying seriously. I'm just
giddy from being in a new country. And here, with
you. And just to be clear, I'm not suggesting the start
of anything serious. It would just be a fling. A one-off.
God, these terms. Can one speak of any of this without
sounding crude? This could be like your pre-wedding,
one-night bachelor party. Do you have such parties
here?

(Beat)

SEIF: I love my fiancée.

JEAN: She's lovely. *(Slight beat)* I thought in case you
were curious before settling down to a perfectly
happy marriage. With all the predictability that
comes with that. Kids, a house. The arguments,
the disappointments—the in-laws, the funeral
arrangements. The end. Something to smile at in
your old age when your kids put you in a home. "I
remember that crazy American tourist. She just started
taking her clothes off, suddenly, in my apartment.
Can you believe it, kids? Barely any warning. Just…
(She removes something.) …started undressing. All she
said was 'anytime you want me to stop just say so and
I will.' No warning. —I could tell some part of her
was mortified by her behavior. She didn't seem to be
having much fun doing it. *(She removes something else, or
just starts unbuttoning a blouse.)* But I could see another
part of her was just daring herself to keep going. Like
she finally had the courage to go out on that rickety
limb. And no sensible reason to stop was going to get
in the way of that. Yes, kids, this happened to your
father." *(She starts to remove another article of clothing.)*

SEIF: Ms Jean. Please. Stop.

(JEAN *freezes. She puts the article of clothing back on. Slight beat.*)

SEIF: I…can not.

JEAN: I understand. Neither can I really.

SEIF: If I was not—

JEAN: If you weren't engaged, I understand. *(Slight beat, then:)* Would you? If you weren't? Make love to me?

SEIF: If I was not…yes.

JEAN: That's very kind of you to say.

SEIF: Not kind. I would want to.

JEAN: Yes? Like…lust? Dare I say?

SEIF: If that is the word for wanting something I can not have, yes…lust.

(Slight beat)

JEAN: Just saying the word alone in a room with a man who isn't my husband is very exciting. I'll take that as a second best to actually making love.

(SEIF *smiles.*)

JEAN: You can't practice safer sex than what just happened. I think I even broke out into a sweat, and my heart was racing. That has to count for something.

SEIF: You are very funny.

JEAN: *(She puts back on whatever else she took off.)* The doorman's right, you can't trust a man and a woman alone in a room.

SEIF: I will take you back to the hotel now.

JEAN: Yes. And…I'm sorry.

SEIF: Do not think of it.

JEAN: About everything that might follow. You don't deserve to be screwed over like this. You're a good man.

SEIF: You did nothing wrong.

JEAN: I'm apologizing for my husband. Coming in with his business deals, flashing his money.

*(*JEAN *gives* SEIF *the letter to read.)*

JEAN: Your fiancé crossing paths with him. I'm sorry for *that.*

SEIF: I don't understand.

JEAN: What does her letter say?

*(*SEIF *reads it.)*

JEAN: I have a sneaky suspicion it's not about how to be a better tour guide…. I'm sorry if it's what I think it is.

(Slight beat as SEIF *reads.)*

JEAN: I thought it might be. What does she say?

SEIF: What do you know of this?

JEAN: I didn't know. Until last night. I was as much in the dark as you. *(Then, a new thought)* If you want to get back at him through me, you're more than welcome to. That didn't sound right. Not now, later. We can screw him over together, later, if that's how you want to play it. None of that sounded right, never mind, ignore everything I just said.

SEIF: We must go.

JEAN: Yes. Of course. Let's go.

(Transitional lights and music)

Scene 7

(MAHA's *bedroom. She is throwing items into a few* suitcases. SEIF *enters. Slight beat as he takes in the suitcases. As before, their exchanges will be in "Arabic", though we will hear them as if in translation.*)

MAHA: I didn't hear the doorbell.

SEIF: Your mother saw me coming from the window. Going somewhere?

MAHA: *(From his expression)* You got the letter. He wasn't supposed to give it to you until tomorrow.

SEIF: Where are you going?

MAHA: Did you read it or didn't you?

(From SEIF's *expression:)*

MAHA: Then why ask.

SEIF: Just like that? Goodbye? Out of thin air? Into thin air?

MAHA: *(Continues packing)* I was—completely—it was a—complete surprise. I had no idea. Last evening he asks to meet for coffee. We meet for coffee. In a coffee shop. And…complete surprise.

SEIF: What was?

MAHA: What he—his—his proposal.

SEIF: He proposed marriage?

MAHA: Can you believe it?

SEIF: Maha.

MAHA: I know,—

SEIF: Could you stop?

MAHA: *(Overlapping)* I'm as—I'm as shocked as you.

SEIF: Could you stop packing for a second?

MAHA: I have to go.

SEIF: If you're as shocked as me can we please talk about how shocked we both are.

MAHA: I don't have time.

SEIF: Maha.

MAHA: There's no time.

SEIF: Maha. This foreigner...this foreigner you showed around last year. He proposes, suddenly, and you start packing?

MAHA: Can you imagine?

SEIF: Stop saying that! No, I can't, that's why I want to talk.

MAHA: I wanted to write a longer letter to explain.

SEIF: So explain now.

MAHA: Seif: I don't want to argue.

SEIF: Oh that's the least you can do for me. A goddamn argument I can understand is the least you can give me.

MAHA: How did your first day as a guide go?

(From SEIF's flabbergasted look:)

MAHA: It's your livelihood now, it's important.

SEIF: First of all—tourists and me? Not a good match. This I know for certain now. And by the way, his wife was there when I read the letter. All day she knew. Everyone knew except me. I'm the donkey in this group. Everyone taking me for a ride: the husband, the wife, and you most of all.

MAHA: I didn't know until last night. Until this morning when I...when I decided.

SEIF: Decided what? When was there something to decide? Please: I promise to be calm, look: even I'm shocked about how calm I am. I'm like, "Wow, good for you Seif. How grown up is this." I feel like I'm in one of those British movies where everyone is being very polite even as they want to scream. All I'm asking before you fly off with this man, I'd like to know why? That's all. If I understand the betrayal then maybe I can take this knife out of my back and stop the bleeding and start the healing.

MAHA: *(Not knowing what to say)* Seif—

SEIF: Can you please stop packing!

(MAHA stops.)

SEIF: I deserve a moment of your time. *(Slight beat)* Do your parents know?

MAHA: I'll tell them when I finish packing.

SEIF: They don't know? —They've no idea? —Wow. They are in for quite the shock. Do it after your father takes his heart medication.

MAHA: Why wouldn't they be happy for me? It's not like they were overjoyed about you. No offense, but you had to know that. You weren't exactly promising a life of security for their daughter.

SEIF: You think they'll be prouder when they find out their daughter is eloping with a married man almost twice her age?

MAHA: When I make something of myself and they see me doing well, yes, maybe, why wouldn't they be? When I start sending them money and supporting them, yes.

SEIF: Did I miss the moment when you became this calculating? Weighing costs/ and benefits—

MAHA: We all do it.

SEIF: *(Continuing)* —or was I always just making excuses for you?

MAHA: We can't all be dreamers like you imagining a married life based on nothing.

SEIF: Love. Based on love. Is that not a thing anymore? Did the stock price on love crash too? Maha, please—

MAHA: You and me, we're—we're like those frogs boiling in water. We really are. Living here, the way it is, the way it's making us a little crazier each day. With everything a monumental pain in the ass and no fun. Where's the fun? The joy in anything? It's like someone took fun and joy and beat them to death. No: it's like someone told fun and joy to go to some government office and get their identity papers in order. And no one's heard from them since. Lost in bureaucracy. And you don't seem bothered. *(She carries on packing.)*

SEIF: So stay and do something about it. You're the one always telling me Egypt will only change if the best and brightest stay and get involved. *I'm* the one who's been saying we should start our life somewhere else.

MAHA: Congratulations, I finally see your point of view. You win.

SEIF: Then leave with me. We'll leave together.

MAHA: And how would that happen?

SEIF: We'll figure it out, like we do everything else.

MAHA: When? With what? How do we get visas? How do we get the money for visas? Money for the plane tickets. Money for when we're there so we don't end up on the streets. Can you answer any of those questions? Just one to get things moving.

SEIF: Now that I know you're serious about emigrating, we'll figure it out.

MAHA: And five years later we'll still be banging our heads against the wall trying to figure it out.

(Slight beat)

SEIF: Why did you want to marry me in the first place if you have such little faith in me?

MAHA: We were kids when we made promises to each other. What did we have to think about? Now the future we thought about is here. I need more than just holding hands on the corniche and dreaming of tomorrow. Tomorrow snuck up on us and here it is slapping us in the face. All the "God-willings" have come round to collect. Even God must be telling us to stop with the "God-willings" and actually do something. How can we help each other now? I stepped aside so you can have this job, what do I get in return? I don't mean that to sound so cold but—

SEIF: You wanted to focus on your designs. That's why we did this, so you can take your first steps into fashion.

MAHA: Is that really why you wanted me to stop?

SEIF: *Yes.*

MAHA: Are you really okay with me having a whole other life apart from you?

SEIF: I've done nothing but encourage you.

MAHA: Your real feelings, Seif. You're not very good at hiding them. Would you really be okay with your wife being a bigger success than you? What rare man can handle that?

SEIF: Again—thank you for believing in me so much you think I can't succeed at anything. Let me digest that for a second. And I would love it if you succeeded. I would be in the front row applauding.

MAHA: Then let me go. Wish me well.

SEIF: With this guy? Go on your own. Wait for me, I'll join you.

MAHA: And what miracle of bureaucracy and finance will make that happen?

(When SEIF *can't answer,* MAHA *resumes packing. Beat)*

SEIF: Do you love him?…Do you even know him?

MAHA: We corresponded.

SEIF: When?

MAHA: Not in a romantic way. Mostly for business. Meetings he wanted me to set up.

SEIF: So you're not in love with him. You're flying off with a man you don't love. *That's* how you want to begin your new life?

MAHA: *(Stops what she's doing)* Paint for me the life we'll have if I stay.

SEIF: We'll do what other couples here do. We'll manage.

MAHA: How many poor married friends do we know who are happy and stay in love? Name me one.

SEIF: Sally and Mahmoud. They're struggling financially, but six years married and they look happier than ever.

MAHA: Sally wants to kill Mahmoud. She complains he's stopped looking for work. All he wants to do is smoke sheesha and play video games.

SEIF: They have problems, sure, but they support each other.

MAHA: Two weeks ago she told me that while they were waiting to cross the street, she felt an overwhelming desire to shove Mahmoud into traffic. She had to hold herself very tight so she wouldn't do it.

SEIF: That's normal. The ups and downs of married life. But they have a commitment to stay together.

MAHA: Seif…your powers of observation are not sharp. (*She resumes packing.*)

SEIF: What is he offering you? What's the deal on the table?

(*When* MAHA *doesn't answer:*)

SEIF: What is it?

MAHA: He says he's madly in love with me.

SEIF: Just like that. Amazing. I want this super power. I want to be an older man with mediocre looks and go up to any young woman and say I love you and suddenly she drops everything and goes with me. Not Superman's power, *that* power. And of course we know where this power (*Makes the gesture for money*) comes from. With cash you can snap your fingers and make people do whatever you want.

MAHA: That's right, I'm a whore. Is there anything else you want to insult me with before I go?

SEIF: I think that's it. That about sums it up, doesn't it?

MAHA: Good. Better we end it like this so I don't feel bad.

(SEIF *walks to the door, ready to exit, but doesn't.* MAHA *continues throwing things into a couple of other smaller suitcases, then stops. Beat*)

SEIF: Maha.

(MAHA *ignores* SEIF.)

SEIF: Maha, look…I get it. (*Slight beat*) Love, not love, I—I get it. It's the smart move. You have ambitions. How can you do what you want here? —Most days Egypt feels like a collapsing life boat. And here comes someone inviting you on to an ocean liner. It would be stupid to ignore the opportunity. And I don't know if I can give you the life you deserve. I'd try but—could I? I don't know if I have that gene, or whatever it is that makes some people super successful. And I don't know if that's me, or this country? Or it's this country telling me it's me when it's really their mess. —I *do* wish you the best. I wanted to marry you didn't I? You think I can just turn that off?…Send postcards…. Actually… don't. Not right away. After you go I will probably hate you for a little while. So—hold off on that. But right now I wish you well.

(Slight beat)

MAHA: This is mad…. This is so mad.

SEIF: It's this country that's crazy town. You, you're making a rational decision. I don't know what century this country lost it, it feels like it's been crazy for years. Maybe it started flipping out with the last Cleopatra. Now there's someone who made bad choices with a foreign guy. *(Realizes he probably shouldn't have said that)* Not that I…

MAHA: I…I can't do this. —It would be a complete scandal.

SEIF: To hell with what people think. Leave while you can. In fact: *(He goes over and starts packing. He puts the remaining items laid out into a suitcase.)* What else are you taking? You can always ask your parents to ship whatever you forget. When's your flight?

MAHA: Tonight. At eleven-thirty.

SEIF: How did you get a visa so fast?

MAHA: He went to university with someone in the embassy.

SEIF: Huh. Connections. Even in America.

MAHA: *Now* you think I should go?

SEIF: You'll suffocate if you stay here. That's what you're saying isn't it? I don't want to be the cause of that. And I *might* end up like Mahmoud, smoking sheesha and you wanting to push me in front of traffic. I don't think I could…I wouldn't be able to take that look in your eyes, seeing me as a failure. I already feel it.

MAHA: I've never thought that.

SEIF: Well, you've kind of said as much.

(Interrupting before she can interject.)

SEIF: It doesn't matter now.

MAHA: I don't, for the record.

SEIF: It's okay. *(Interrupting before she can interject)* Okay, you don't.

(Slight beat)

MAHA: Really? …"Go Maha, good luck"?

(SEIF nods.)

MAHA: And what about you? —What do you do?

SEIF: You think I can't manage without you. After you leave and I collapse into a depression and start taking drugs I'll—I'll be fine. Better than fine: I'll join you in America. What do you think of that? *And:* I'll win you back. Yup. I'll get a job driving a cab, earn money and marry you. You'll end up being embarrassed, of course, introducing your husband as a cab driver and eventually divorce me. Which will traumatize the children we'll have had by then. But. And. I'll probably remarry, you'll remarry. Then we'll bump into each other again in that big park in New York in our sixties and realize there really is no one else in the whole world for us but each other. We'll divorce our spouses and marry again—with our children giving us away. Who'll be deep in therapy by then. And we'll live happily ever after.

(Slight beat)

MAHA: Could happen.

SEIF: I'm counting on it.

MAHA: And Egypt? ...I just leave? —Walk away from everything? My responsibilities? I'd be such a hypocrite.

SEIF: Is there a committee that would applaud you for staying? Even the remaining protestors would tell you to get out. Can you believe they're still protesting after all these years? They were outside the museum while we were there.

MAHA: Good for them.

SEIF: You? Ms Status Quo? I-wish-the-revolution-had-never-happened? That's new.

MAHA: Something has to change. Or we're all going to explode—*again*.

SEIF: Well they're not going to do it. We saw what happened last time.

MAHA: That doesn't mean they shouldn't keep trying.

SEIF: This *is* new for you. —Perhaps I should join them instead of flying off to you. I help stage the next revolution, but this time we win long term because I'll *really* get involved. I'll help put in place new laws that make everything better, which will make you want to come back and start your fashion empire right here.

MAHA: Okay...that sounds like a better plan. —I can see you in politics. Now that you say it.

SEIF: Because I'm opinionated and have a big mouth?

MAHA: For those very qualities, yes. I think it would suit you.

SEIF: Just remember to send food packages when they haul me off to prison.

(MAHA *goes over and kisses* SEIF. *It's held for a little while. They break. She looks at him.*)

MAHA: I really do think it would suit you.

(SEIF *smiles.*)

SEIF: Us. I think it would suit us. (*Gesturing as if seeing the slogan*) "Elect Maha and Seif. The Best Tour Guides For A Better Egypt." Or: "For A Better Egyptian Tomorrow: Maha And Seif". —Or something like that.

MAHA: (*Slight beat, smiling*) Or something like that.

(MAHA *and* SEIF *look at each other as lights and music transition to:*)

Scene 8

(JEAN *and* PAUL's *hotel room. He enters with his suitcase. He stands there a few beats. He notices her open, packed suitcase. She enters from the bathroom wearing a summery dress. She is zipping up a toiletry bag which she will place in her suitcase. She stops when she sees him.*)

JEAN: (*Surprised*) Oh. Hello.

PAUL: You're leaving?

JEAN: I am.

PAUL: You're flying back already?

JEAN: I'm checking into another hotel.

PAUL: Why? This one's paid for. —Which hotel?

JEAN: I don't know yet. I thought I'd ask the concierge. I'll tell him I'm looking for a cheaper place so he doesn't get offended. Or I may start looking for an apartment. It can't be that difficult can it? Do you know how long we can stay with the visas we have?

PAUL: You're thinking of hanging out longer?

JEAN: There's so much to see. That museum alone. I could spend days and days just wandering through its halls.

PAUL: You went with Seif?

JEAN: I did.

PAUL: How, er—? How is he?

JEAN: You mean after he found out you're running off with his fiancée?

PAUL: You told him?

JEAN: Maha. In a letter. Aren't you supposed to be flying out with her this evening?

PAUL: She...never showed up. —Never picked up when I called. Just—sent a text: "I'm not coming. Good luck. Goodbye." *(He looks shell-shocked.)*

JEAN: Oh...I'm sorry. That must have hit hard.

PAUL: Jean...I've made a mistake. I don't know what I was thinking.

JEAN: You were very clear about what you were thinking. *(She puts any other remaining items of hers into the suitcase. She will close the bag when finished.)*

PAUL: I made a stupid—stupid mistake. I lost my mind for a moment. A day. One day. My mind took a one-day excursion and got lost in a very—strange—mental place where it had no business going.

JEAN: You should have just bought a red sports car when you got home. That's supposed to do the trick for some men, apparently.

PAUL: Leaving you? The most gorgeous woman I know. I'm an idiot.

JEAN: Now that I think of it, I wonder if that's why baboons have such red asses when aroused. I just made the connection. It's amazing how desire will lower a man's IQ. I'd like to be fair and say it affects both sexes, but men seem really adept at becoming stupid when sexually aroused. But you're only human.

PAUL: I am. It's no excuse, but.

JEAN: It isn't, no.

PAUL: I went blind for a *very* brief second. I'd miss everything about you, and the wonderful life we've built. Maybe I—I needed this moment of madness to appreciate everything we have. And we have—so much. Our life, together. It's so—rich, in so many ways. You can't trade that in. Not—I don't mean you, trade you in, I mean this history we share. All the good times we've had together, even the bad times. Living with you...how could I even think to throw that away.

JEAN: But you did. You did throw it away.

PAUL: And I will never forgive myself for that.

JEAN: You know I was just giving myself a good look-over in the mirror. A real, take-no-prisoners stare at my body, and you know what: it's not all gone.

PAUL: None of it's gone.

JEAN: Well some of it's gone.

PAUL: Nothing that matters.

JEAN: That sounds faintly insulting.

PAUL: *No.* All the different kinds of wonderful that's you are still there.

JEAN: You'll say you love me for my personality next.

PAUL: I don't know how I can unsay what I said. I don't know how I can walk back the sheer dumbness of...I can't even say it was a decision. It was a crazy dash to—I've no idea where. I don't know what possessed me, or where I thought I was going. Maybe

it was the heat? Can we just say blame it on the heat?
Please?

JEAN: *(As she finishes packing)* I get it. I do. We all dream
of escape. Nothing mysterious about that. Most lives
get boring eventually, don't they? The sheer—numbing
repetition of, well—just about everything. This one
life we work so hard to get right. It really is quite cruel
when you think about it. Because nothing you do is
ever satisfactory enough, is it. The security you crave
becomes contemptible, eventually, and no security is
unacceptable. I don't know why people fantasize about
immortality, we can barely get through this life.

PAUL: Jean—can you...can you please forgive me?

JEAN: Thank you for this, by the way. *(She's touching the
necklace she's wearing.)* It's lovely.

PAUL: It looks great on you.

JEAN: What's it called again?

PAUL: An "ankh".

JEAN: I was trying to look it up. It's a pharaonic symbol
for something. Life? Afterlife?

PAUL: I wanted to get you something special for our
anniversary.

JEAN: Maha has great taste. Thank you. *(She is all packed
and ready to leave.)*

PAUL: What do you want me to do? How can I make
up for a moment of—just—because that's all it was, a
stupid blip in an otherwise pretty damn solid marriage.
Right?

JEAN: Well—the iceberg that sunk the Titanic was a
stupid blip in the scale of things.

PAUL: Jean. *(Gets on one knee)* You know how bad my
knees are. I may never get up again. Please: forgive me.
Let's fly back home together.

JEAN: There's nothing to forgive. I should be thanking you. I had no idea I needed to be free of you. Even more years may have passed before I'd realized that. Thank you for helping me not waste even more time. And like Maha said: good luck. Sincerely. I mean that.

(JEAN *starts to exit, but then stops and pushes* PAUL's *wheeled suitcase so that it rolls over to him.*)

JEAN: To help you get up.

PAUL: We can still make this work, I know it. I'll work my ass off to make the rest of our lives amazing. Give me the chance to prove myself again to you.

JEAN: Making my life amazing is not your responsibility. It's mine. Now get off your knee before it locks. (*She heads for the door.*)

PAUL: Wait.

(JEAN *stops at the door.*)

PAUL: Are you really going out in that dress?

(JEAN *looks at* PAUL. *Then exits. Lights and music transition to:*)

Scene 9

(*On the felucca as before.* JEAN *is seated in the boat with her suitcase. She now has a shawl wrapped around her shoulders. The same* BOATMAN *at the stern holding the tiller. Gentle sounds of water. Beat.*)

JEAN: Do you speak English? At all? …Even a little bit?

(*The* BOATMAN *gives a thumbs up sign.*)

JEAN: You don't. That's okay. I'm sure nothing said in my language can't be said much better in yours. I wanted to apologize for the other day. I was being rude—thinking you were staring at me. As if. How arrogant of me. Mixed in with a little… shyness? I'm so glad you don't understand English.

BOATMAN: *(Gestures towards the sunset, the Nile)* Beautiful.

JEAN: Yes. —The light—on the water. —This boat…

(The BOATMAN smiles. In the next section, she switches from addressing him, to musing to herself, and out to her surroundings:)

JEAN: No husband this time. Or ever again. I'm free. —Or lost. Mostly free. Or let loose? I think there's a difference, isn't there? —I think freedom takes a little harder work. But right now I'm footloose and…that feels great. A little frightening. Mostly frightening. But that's also thrilling. How wonderful to just set sail, into the damn sunset for goodness sake. *On the Nile.* *(A laugh)* Which myth is it? Greek or Egyptian, where the ferryman takes you across the river after you die? I think it's Greek. Except this is the opposite of that…. What is your name? *(Touching her chest)* Jean. My name is Jean. Yours is? *(Points to him)*

BOATMAN: Abdallah.

JEAN: Hello Abdallah.

BOATMAN: Hello.

JEAN: *(A laugh)* I really hope you don't understand me—with me yammering away about my—silly… *(She remembers the ring on her finger.)* Oh. Reminds me.

(JEAN removes her ring, looks at it, then tosses it into the Nile. We hear a little splash.)

JEAN: Won't be needing that.

(The BOATMAN looks startled by her action, ready to jump in)

JEAN: No/ no.

BOATMAN: Madame?

JEAN: *(Holds her hand up to prevent him from jumping in)*
I meant to do it. Glad to be rid of it. Though I should
have given it to you, shouldn't I. You could've sold it
or something. —Oh well. I promise to give you a big
tip. And who knows, maybe it will bring me good luck.
Like throwing coins in that Italian fountain. Or was
that just a movie thing? —Throwing your wedding
ring in the Nile has to count for something. *(Beat)* I
have led a very useless life, Abdallah. —Except I don't
know if the life I could have had would've been any
better. The moments of feeling great as a mother, a
wife…they've really not been enough. Not close to
enough. And now I've no idea what I'm supposed
to do to make up for that. I feel so—rotten. Rotting,
actively, like those—all those things I should have
taken care of, *(Touches her chest)* for me, kept alive,
instead of letting it all—*rot*. And now I don't know
how to bring any of it back. I want to scream most
of the time like I can't take my next breath without
wanting to let something out that's very—loud….
But I promise I won't, again. —All I know for sure is
I would like to be…loved. In some small way. And I
don't know how I can make that happen. You can't
force someone to love you. I know all the self-help
books would tell me to do it on my own. Find the love
within. Except right now I'd settle for something much
simpler. Like being held. I don't remember being held
in a way that made me feel—anything. Even like I was
being held. *(Caught in the thought for a moment. Then:)*
I'm sorry for going on about myself. God knows what
problems you're going through. But I just…I know
there's so much more out there, and I've barely lived
any of it…. Any of it. *(Slight beat. She takes out the map.)*
How far is it to Luxor? How crazy would it be if we

sailed all the way down to Luxor? We could pick up food supplies along the way.

BOATMAN: Ms Jean.

JEAN: *(Surprised she's being addressed)* Yes?…Yes?

BOATMAN: *(Gestures to take in their surroundings)* Beautiful.

JEAN: Yes, it most certainly is.

BOATMAN: Like you.

(This affects JEAN. She didn't expect it. She looks at the BOATMAN to see if it was said to be polite, or if he was trying to bridge some divide. He looks at her. His demeanor seems sincere, compassionate. Slight beat)

JEAN: Thank you for that. *(Slight beat)* Thank you for that. *(Slight beat. She looks out.)* Tonight…I think I will be.

(Slight beat. The lights dim to night and stars, reflected in the sky and water. Hold to the sound of lapping water. Blackout)

END OF PLAY

www.ingramcontent.com/pod-product-compliance
Lightning Source LLC
Chambersburg PA
CBHW052209090426
42741CB00010B/2475